About Asia Society

Preparing Asians and Americans for a shared future

Asia Society is the leading global and pan-Asian organization working to strengthen relationships and promote understanding among the people, leaders, and institutions of the United States and Asia. We seek to increase knowledge and enhance dialogue, encourage creative expression, and generate new ideas across the fields of arts and culture, policy and business, and education.

Founded in 1956, Asia Society is a nonpartisan, nonprofit educational institution with offices in Hong Kong, Houston, Los Angeles, Manila, Melbourne, Mumbai, New York, San Francisco, Seoul, Shanghai, and Washington, DC.

2011 Asian Pacific Americans Corporate Survey:

New Perspectives on Engaging APA Employees

Thank you to all our sponsors:

2011 APA Corporate Survey Research Sponsors

Lead sponsor:

nationalgrid
The power of action.

Silver sponsors:

CardinalHealth Essential to care™

GE

PEPSICO

Supporters of the 2011 Survey Report

citi   **CORNING**   **Goldman Sachs**   **MasterCard** Worldwide   **PEPSICO**   **TimeWarner**

Special thanks to those who helped support and guide this survey and report to completion:

Senior Advisor
> **Philip A. Berry**, President, Philip Berry Associates LLC
> Author: Being Better Than You Believe:8 Steps to Ultimate Success

Survey Steering Committee
> **Deborah Turner Bailey**, Global Diversity Officer, Human Resource Director, Global Staff and Business Services, Corning Incorporated
> **Maurice Cox**, Vice President, Corporate Development & Diversity, PepsiCo
> **Geraldine Gallashaw**, Head of Global Diversity Strategy, BNY Mellon
> **Neddy Perez**, Vice President, Diversity & Inclusion, Ingersoll-Rand
> **Aida Sabo**, Vice President, Diversity and Inclusion, Cardinal Health
> **Amy Shang**, Managing Director, HSBC
> **Todd Sears**, Founder, Coda, LLC

Survey Production Team
> **David Reid**, Director of Corporate Relations, Asia Society
> **Mike Kulma**, Executive Director, Global Leadership Initiatives, Asia Society
> **Jonathan Saw**, Project Manager, Asian Pacific Americans Corporate Survey, Asia Society
> **Anna Erickson**, Director of Consulting Services, Questar - Global Survey Research

Asia Society Corporate Diversity Council as of September 2011

Purpose of the Council: To advise Asia Society on how best to leverage its public voice in the area of diversity leadership and how to best serve Corporate Members with their global leadership objectives. The Council provides a regular forum for members to share best practices on the leadership challenges they face in the US and Asia.

Diversity Council Co-Chairs

Ron Glover
Vice President,
Diversity & Workforce Policy
IBM

Stephanie N. Mehta
Executive Editor
Fortune Magazine

Nereida Perez
Vice President,
Diversity & Inclusion
Ingersoll Rand

Rohini Anand
Senior Vice President
Global Chief Diversity Officer
Sodexo

Letty Ashworth
Manager Global Diversity
Delta Air Lines, Inc.

Subha Barry*
SVP, Chief Diversity Officer
Freddie Mac

Anthony Carter
VP, Global Diversity & Inclusion,
Chief Diversity Officer
Johnson & Johnson

Jyoti Chopra
Managing Director
Global Communications
Deloitte Touche Tohmatsu Limited

Marianne Churchwell
Vice President, Human Resources
Lear Corporation

Maurice Cox
Vice President
Corporate Development & Diversity
PepsiCo.

Deborah Dagit
Chief Diversity Officer
Merck & Co.

Manolet G. Dayrit
Partner
KPMG LLP

Ana Duarte-McCarthy
Chief Diversity Officer
Citigroup

Deborah Elam
Chief Diversity Officer
GE

Edward Gadsden
SVP & Chief Diversity Officer
Pfizer Inc.

Michelle Gadsden-Williams
Managing Director
Global Head of Diversity & Inclusion
Credit Suisse

Geraldine Gallashaw
Head of Global Diversity Strategy
BNY Mellon

Aynesh Johnson
VP, Global Leadership & Diversity
Goldman, Sachs & Co.

Donna Johnson
Chief Diversity Officer
MasterCard Worldwide

Eugene Kelly
Worldwide Director,
Global Diversity & Inclusion
Colgate-Palmolive Company

Kathryn Komsa
Vice President, Diversity & Inclusion
Marsh & McLennan Companies, Inc.

Denice Kronau
Chief Diversity Officer
Siemens

Lance A. LaVergne
Vice President &
Chief Diversity Officer
New York Life Insurance Company

Lisa Mink
Executive Director,
Global Diversity and Inclusion
Dell

Jimmie Paschall
Senior Vice President
Global Diversity Officer
Marriott International

Aida Sabo
Vice President
Diversity & Inclusion
Cardinal Health

Amy Shang
Managing Director
HSBC

Jeffrey Siminoff
Managing Director,
Head of Global Inclusion
Morgan Stanley

Marva Smalls
Executive Vice President Global
Inclusion Strategy
MTV Networks

Barbara Stern
Director of Global Personnel
& Talent Management
McKinsey & Company

Geri Thomas
SVP, Global Diversity & Inclusion
Executive and Georgia Market President
Bank of America

Debra Turner Bailey
Global Diversity Officer
Human Resource Director
Corning Incorporated

Ali Walji
Vice President & Diversity Officer
Chartis

Melinda Wolfe
Head of Professional Development
Bloomberg

Advisors:
Vishakha N. Desai
President
Asia Society

Philip A. Berry*
President
Philip Berry Assoc. LLC

Michael E. Chen
President, Strategic Initiatives Group
NBC News

Ted Childs
Principal
Ted Childs LLC

J.D. Hokoyama
President & CEO
LEAP

Todd Sears
Principal
Coda LLC

* indicates Founding Co-Chairs

Table of Contents

Introduction

Asia Society began conducting the Asian Pacific Americans Corporate Survey to address the need for independent information, backed by statistics, about the Asian Pacific American (APA) workforce. At that time, in 2010, there was very little information about APA employees and their perceptions and experiences working at Fortune 500-level companies.

The Asia Society's Corporate Diversity Council, a group made up of over 25 corporate diversity officers from Fortune 500 companies, was critical in providing the support and strategic guidance for developing the survey. In addition to reporting the data from the survey, we have also created a resource for companies to learn about best practices for APA-focused diversity efforts, from training and development to activities with direct effect on a company's bottom line.

Last year, the APA Corporate Survey report highlighted what it took to become a Best in Class employer for APAs. This year, our data highlights new perspectives on how best to achieve APA engagement, including a very provocative finding centered on the amount of time one has lived in the U.S.

As many experts in diversity know, sometimes programs to engage APA employees are based on a broad brush approach – assuming the existence of a pan-Asian sensibility on which to develop programs and other engagement activities. At other times, the approaches address the diversity that exists within the community by basing programming on perceived differences in the APA employees' countries of origin.

Data from the 2011 Asia Society APA Corporate Survey suggest that these approaches may be addressing only part of the overall APA engagement environment. It seems that the longer an APA employee has been in the U.S., the less favorably they view each of the dimensions studied. After about 11-15 years in the United States, favorability scores on many dimensions decrease to below 50% – especially Professional Growth and Development and Leadership.

According to U.S. 2010 Census figures, 76% of Asian Americans were either born here or have been here for over 11 years. Given that it is these two groups that provide the lowest favorability scores in the survey, it would seem that less than 50% of the vast majority of APAs have a favorable view of professional growth and development at their companies.

These APA Americans, like all Americans, simply expect more. Regardless of country of origin, these employees may be best positioned to perceive where Corporate America's formal policies and commitment to diversity are not fully realized on the day-to-day level. It may be this dichotomy that is showing up in the lower overall favorability scores these employees give their companies. On the other hand, APAs who have arrived here more recently are singularly focused on establishing a foothold both economically and culturally in the US – similar to immigrants of any ethnicity. One could make the case that beyond overt discriminatory practices – which are both illegal and rare – these APA employees may be satisfied with current structures and programs.

The data suggest that efforts to engage APA employees need to include "time in the U.S." as an additional filter through which to address their needs and concerns in the workplace. We can hypothesize that this approach may be fruitful for engaging the APA marketplace as well.

APAs are the second fastest growing ethnic group in the United States. In fact, the 2010 U.S. Census shows that those who identified their race as "Asian alone," which does not include Pacific Islanders, were the fastest growing ethnic/racial group. Thus, understanding the differences in the APA community beyond the old-school country-based classifications will be paramount for engaging APA employees, and for success in the growing APA market. In addition, with the economic rise of Asia overall, and China and India specifically, the mere fact that the U.S. has a talent pool that understands this fast-growing part of the world will be a critical competitive advantage.

To fully realize this opportunity, companies need to ensure that the contributions of APA employees are not devalued. The findings in this report suggest an overall pathway to realizing the full potential of Asian Pacific American employees, the APA market, and the growing Asian markets. But making the findings relevant within a company's specific business and corporate culture is where real change and evolution will happen.

— Vishakha N. Desai, President, Asia Society

BACKGROUND AND METHODOLOGY

Background and Methodology

Asia Society first conducted the Asian Pacific Americans Corporate Survey in 2010, at which time it was the first survey to exclusively measure and recognize practices related to developing Asian Pacific Americans working at Fortune 500-level companies. The 2011 Asian Pacific Americans Corporate Survey was conducted in order to provide both quantitative and qualitative information on the APA employee base.

Asia Society partnered with Questar, a third-party survey vendor, to facilitate a two-part evaluation process. In one part, a targeted employee survey provided APA employees with an opportunity to communicate their experiences around how well their company develops and promotes Asian Pacific American employees, and how well it supports APA culture and community. Simultaneously, Corporate Diversity Officers from each participating company described the programs, policies, and activities they are most excited about that support Asian Pacific American employees.

The Asia Society's 2011 Asian Pacific Americans Corporate Survey process included responses from thousands of Asian Pacific American employees from the ranks of the Fortune 500 and similar-sized companies. The employee survey measured key dimensions of the work environment for Asian Pacific American employees, including *Leadership and Company Image*, *Professional Growth & Development*, *Involvement in the Asian Pacific American Community*, *Diversity*, *The Job Itself*, and *Overall Satisfaction*.

Throughout the report, results are examined in the context of employee engagement. Companies that are able to attract, retain, and develop engaged employees see less turnover, higher quality products, and greater customer satisfaction. With diversity comes a number of unique considerations for engaging employees. The results of the survey help uncover some of these considerations for APA employees.

KEY FINDINGS

Length of time in the U.S. May Be a Critical Asian Pacific American (APA) Distinction

Favorability scores for all six dimensions generally decrease in inverse proportion to an employee's length of time in the United States. Asian Pacific American employees who have *more recently moved* to the United States tend to see their employer *more positively* when compared with those who have lived in the United States longer.

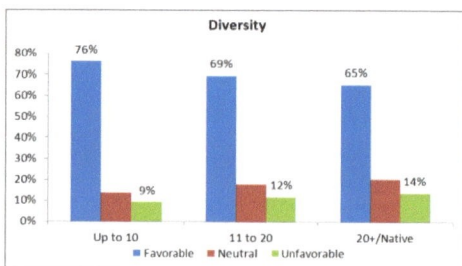

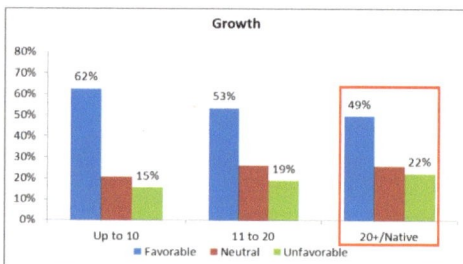

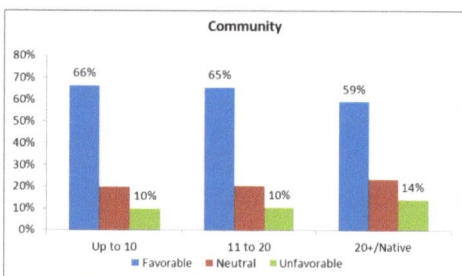

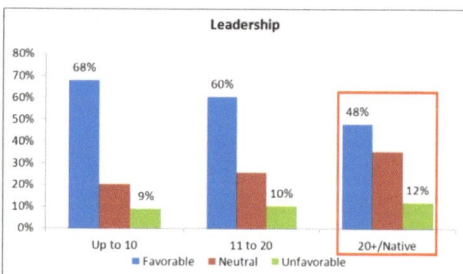

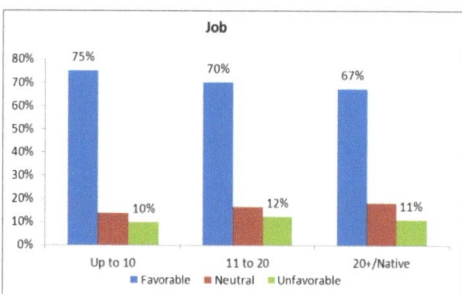

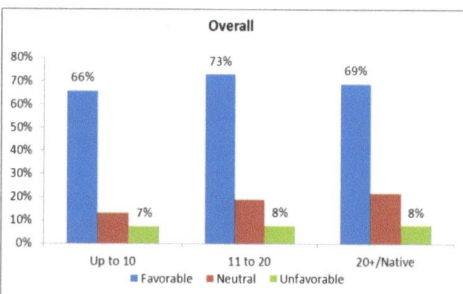

Dimension favorability in % by years in US
Red boxes highlight areas below 50% favorability

In fact, observed differences between countries of origin may be partly explained by time in the US. For example, our study indicates that APA employees of Chinese descent view their companies less favorably than employees of Indian descent.

However, taking a closer look at the respondents, 60% of the Chinese heritage group have been in the US 20+ years, compared to only 43% of those with Indian heritage, which could at least partially explain the lower favorability scores overall.

While the differences do not disappear, adding the "time in U.S." factor presents a much more complex situation. This calls for a more nuanced approach toward employee engagement, and also suggests that marketing and other external outreach to the APA community needs to take this factor into account as well.

APA employees remain highly engaged and committed to company success

A strong majority of Asian Pacific Americans who responded to the survey indicated that they really care about seeing their company succeed (89%), suggesting feelings of loyalty to the organization. However, survey respondents strongly feel that their employers could do a better job of promoting APAs into senior leadership positions (leadership & company image) as well as provide better growth and development opportunities tailored to APAs (professional growth & development).

Development opportunities, ability to reach full potential, ability to employ unique skill sets, and being recognized for strengths are the top APA employee engagement drivers

APA employees who feel good about their development opportunities feel a greater sense of belonging, and are more committed to company success, less likely to leave, and more likely to recommend their employer to other APAs as a great place to work.

"Best in Class" employers differ significantly from other Finalist companies on a number of topics

Among the strongest differences are participation in employee resource groups (83% vs. 56%), mentoring opportunities that are specifically tailored for Asian Pacific Americans (67% vs. 40%), and offering of expatriate or international assignments in Asia (68% vs. 45%). And although the favorability percentage could be higher, "Best in Class" employers are also significantly more likely to promote APAs into senior leadership than the other companies we surveyed (57% vs. 36%).

Six Best Practice Areas emerged that differentiate Finalist companies from other employers

These are 1) leveraging of employee resource groups, 2) tailoring career development for APA employees, 3) creating a sense of belonging in the workplace, 4) outstanding support for family and community, 5) encouraging employees to pursue opportunities in Asia, and 6) supporting workplace flexibility. Employees also offered further suggestions on how to make an organization a great place for Asian Pacific Americans to work.

BEST IN CLASS AND FINALIST COMPANIES

A Closer Look at Best in Class and Finalist Companies

Finalist companies were selected by Questar, according to a statistical analysis of the scores from the employee survey for each company.

Best in Class companies were selected among the finalists using a weighted formula. Eighty percent of the final score came from the employee survey responses. Twenty percent of the final score was determined by a judging panel, comprised of five experts in diversity leadership. Each panel member reviewed submissions from each finalist. Company identification information was concealed from the panel members in order to ensure objectivity in ratings. Scores were based on a number of factors; such as the gap between corporate policies/programming (as evidenced by the application form that was completed by the company's diversity leadership) and actual APA employee experiences (as measured by the scores given by employees of the company who took the survey.)

To maintain the integrity of the scoring, Asia Society staff played no role in the judging process.

This year's competition proved challenging due to the number of outstanding companies that qualified as finalists. The 20 finalists, highly regarded Fortune 500 and similar companies from a variety of industries, each possessed a notably strong Asian Pacific American diversity focus.

Best in Class

Award Finalists
(in alphabetical order)

3M	KPMG LLP
Cardinal Health, Inc.	Kraft Foods
Cisco	Lear Corporation
Colgate-Palmolive Company	McDonald's Corporation
Corning Incorporated	New York Life Insurance Company
Freddie Mac	PepsiCo, Inc.
GE	Pfizer
Goldman, Sachs & Co.	PG&E Corporation
HSBC Bank	Sodexo
Kaiser Permanente	Time Warner Inc.

Best in Class Comparisons
Growth and Leadership Dimensions Set Best in Class Apart

How do the 2011 Best in Class companies compare to the rest? Differences between the Best in Class and other companies we surveyed were examined to identify areas where distinctions arise.

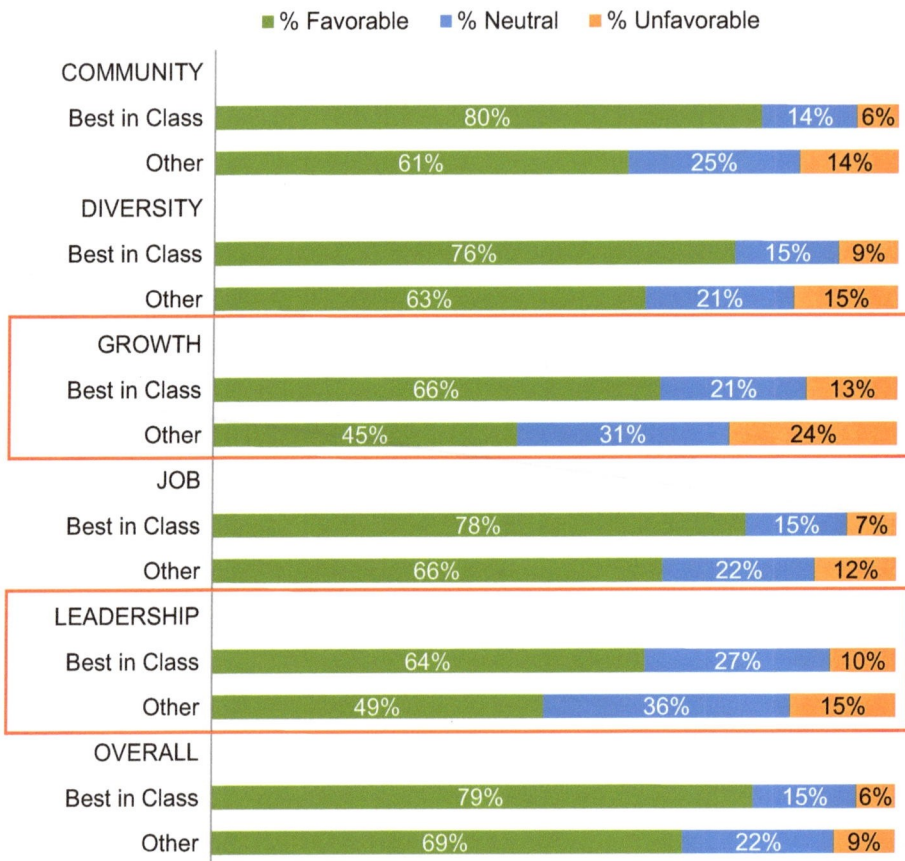

The Best in Class companies received higher survey scores across the board. However, in the dimensions of Growth and Leadership – which are of critical importance for APA employees – Best in Class companies really shine. These dimensions received favorability scores of less than 50% for other companies, but Best in Class received scores in the 60% range.

For Best in Class, Growth and Leadership Take Many Forms

QUESTION	BEST IN CLASS	OTHERS	DIFFERENCE
Participation in APA groups	83%	56%	+27
Mentoring tailored to APAs	67%	40%	+27
International assignments	57%	34%	+23
APA role models	68%	45%	+23
APAs in senior leadership	57%	36%	+21
Networking opportunities	86%	67%	+19
APA community ties	62%	43%	+19
Company supports APA groups	83%	65%	+18
APA involvement in engaging Asian customers	58%	41%	+17
Promotion fairness	74%	56%	+18
Positive company image in APA community	77%	60%	+17
Sense of belonging	69%	52%	+17

A closer look at the various dimensions elucidates just how Best in Class companies provide for Growth and Leadership.

The chart above shows the specific items with the greatest differences between Best in Class employers and other employers. Among these items, Best in Class companies have greater **participation in APA groups**, more **networking opportunities with other APAs,** and greater **support for APA groups**, as well as higher **involvement in the APA community** outside of the company.

Initiatives such as these support companies in actively building an environment of inclusion that allows employees to focus on their individual strengths rather than cultural differences. By publicly demonstrating support for APA employees through formal Employee Resource Groups, and by supporting the APA community outside the company, organizations communicate the importance of their APA employees and the contributions that they make. By providing formal networking opportunities, organizations provide employees with a support system that can help individuals navigate job and career challenges.

In addition to the increased support for networking that Best in Class employers provide for their APA employees, these employers were also more likely to provide support for *professional growth & development.* APA employees within these companies were more likely to see growth opportunities that were specific to them as APAs. For example, Best in Class employers received higher ratings for providing opportunities for *international assignments*, *APA role models,* and having *APAs in senior leadership positions*. With the growing importance of talent management and retention of top talent within many organizations today, it is important that APAs see opportunities for career growth if their employers hope to recruit and retain this important source of talent. In fact, research shows that perceived opportunity for career growth is a key driver, not only for employee retention, but also for employee engagement. Employees who believe there are opportunities for their own growth and development work harder, are more committed, and are more likely to stay with their employer when compared with employees who do not see those opportunities. International assignments have been shown to be one of the most developmental types of assignments in preparing individuals for leadership. By tying these opportunities to cultural learning, employers can leverage individual strengths of APA employees to get the most from the assignment – for both employer and employee.

Best in Class Companies Continue to Get Better

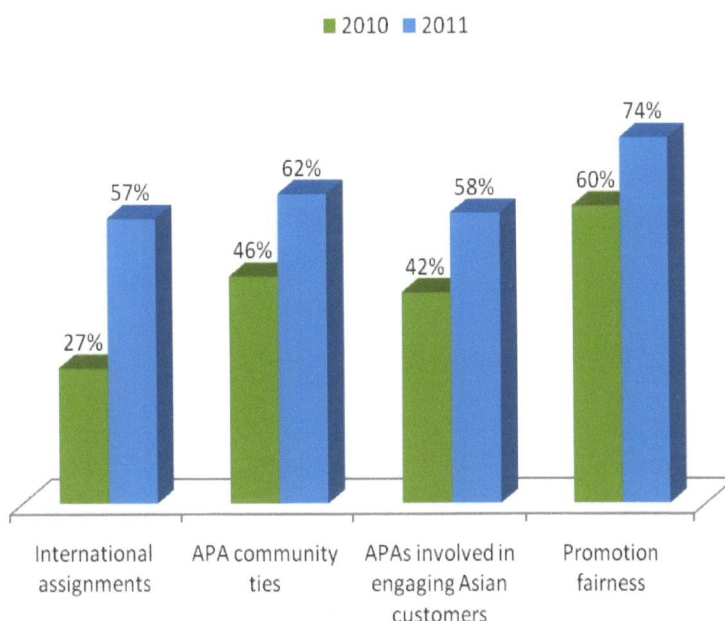

Legend: ■ 2010 ■ 2011

Chart values:
- International assignments: 27% (2010), 57% (2011)
- APA community ties: 46% (2010), 62% (2011)
- APAs involved in engaging Asian customers: 42% (2010), 58% (2011)
- Promotion fairness: 60% (2010), 74% (2011)

From 2010 to 2011, several survey items showed large increases in scores. These areas ranged from *international assignments*, where there was a 30% increase in scores when compared with 2010, to *promotion fairness*, with a 14% increase. These results show the many-faceted ways in which Best in Class companies support and develop APA employees.

While many organizations have pulled away from the traditional expatriate assignment because of the cost, Best in Class employers see the value in getting their employees into these markets – gaining cultural experience firsthand by working overseas. As globalization changes the competitive landscape, Best in Class employers understand the value of true preparation for leading globally. International assignments bring not only challenge and growth for employees, but also competitive advantages for companies that use them strategically.

Employees working for the 2011 Best in Class companies also feel that their company has *strong ties to the APA community* (16% increase) and that their *company utilizes APA employees to*

engage Asian customers (16% increase), more than they did last year. The image that employees have of their employer, and the support that they feel, goes beyond internal programs and communications. Employee engagement and commitment are also impacted by the way an employer is perceived among family and friends. Through support for the APA community and leveraging employees to understand customers, Best in Class employers have the potential to increase sales while driving employee engagement and loyalty.

Driving APA Employee Engagement

Companies benefit greatly from attracting, retaining, and developing an engaged workforce. Employee engagement has gained much attention in the popular press and professional literature in recent years. The concept is unique in its focus on work outcomes rather than employee satisfaction or well-being. Through more than 20 years of research, employee engagement has emerged as critical to building an effective and productive organization. Employees who are engaged are highly motivated, energetic, focused on work, committed to the organization, and willing to put in extra effort to accomplish work-related goals. Research has demonstrated a clear link between employee engagement and key business outcomes such as customer loyalty, service quality, productivity, and employee retention.

In order to understand employee engagement for Asian Pacific American employees, regression-based ***Relative Weights Analysis***[1] was used to identify the Top 10 drivers of employee engagement for APA employees based on 2011 survey results. Results of this analysis are displayed in rank order in the table below.

---

[1] Johnson, J. W. (2001). Determining the relative importance of predictors in multiple regression: Practical applications of relative weights. In F. Columbus (Ed.), *Advances in psychology research*, Vol. 5 (pp. 231-251). Hauppauge, NY: Nova Science.

Top Driver

Top 10 Drivers of APA Employee Engagement (Ranked by order of importance)
#1 Development opportunities
#2 Ability to reach full potential
#3 Ability to employ unique skill sets
#4 Recognized for strengths
#5 Support for leadership development
#6 Flexible work arrangements
#7 Promotion fairness
#8 Respectful work environment
#9 Positive company image in APA community
#10 Commitment to diversity

Five of the top 10 drivers of engagement among APAs focused on support for career development, including feeling good about opportunities for career growth, recognition for strengths, utilizing their skills, and reaching their potential. These results indicate that employees who felt good about their career opportunities might be more likely to

- care about the future of the company
- feel a sense of belonging at work
- recommend their employer as a good place to work to other APAs
- remain with their employer if offered another comparable job

Other important factors driving these employee engagement outcomes included perceptions of flexibility, fairness, respectfulness, and support for diversity, as well as the employer's reputation within the APA community.

Work Still Needs to be done in APA Personal Development and Recognition

Although most engagement drivers were similar between Best in Class employers and other employers, some differences did emerge. For example, **flexible work arrangements** and *a **respectful work environment*** are more important to driving employee engagement among employees from the Best in Class employers, while **career development opportunities** are more important drivers for employees at other companies. (In the following chart, items in italics are those that are not in the other group's top 10.)

Best in Class Top 10 Drivers of Employee Engagement	All Others Top 10 Drivers of Employee Engagement
#1 Flexible work arrangements	#1 Development opportunities
#2 Respectful work environment	#2 Ability to reach full potential
#3 Development opportunities	#3 Ability to employ unique skill sets
#4 Ability to reach full potential	#4 Recognized for strengths
#5 Support for leadership development	#5 Support for leadership development
#6 Recognized for strengths	#6 Promotion fairness
#7 Ability to employ unique skill sets	#7 Flexible work arrangements
#8 Commitment to diversity	#8 Positive company image in APA community
#9 Strategies for growth in Asian markets	#9 Respectful work environment
#10 Networking opportunities	#10 Commitment to diversity

Looking at the relative importance of engagement drivers concerned with personal development and recognition (boxed in red above), we see that four of the top five drivers for other companies are in these areas, as opposed to just two for Best in Class companies. This could indicate a perception among employees of non-Best in Class companies that their employers have not effectively addressed these issues. At the same time, Best in Class companies still need to address these drivers, as they remain in the top 10 for their employees as well.

BEST PRACTICES FOR
SUPPORTING ASIA PACIFIC AMERICAN
EMPLOYEES

Best Practices for Supporting Asian Pacific American Employees

Companies that support their APAs best do so through outstanding and innovative programs and processes. Each finalist company was interviewed to better understand the best practices and emerging trends in creating an environment that best supports APA employees. Best practices aligned with survey findings around Best in Class characteristics and fell into 6 categories:

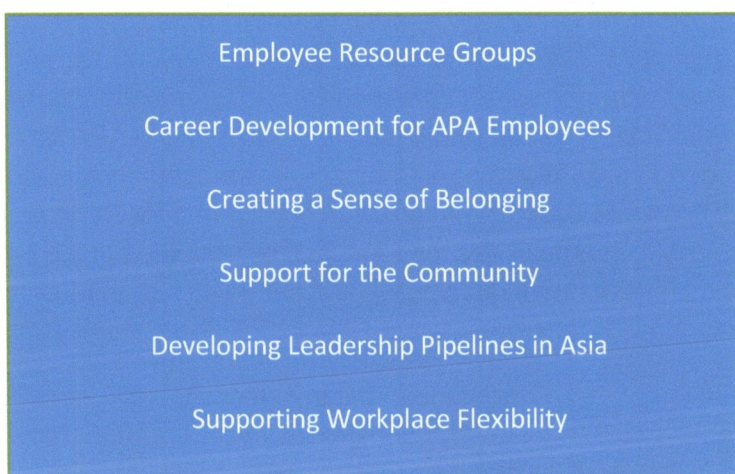

> Employee Resource Groups
>
> Career Development for APA Employees
>
> Creating a Sense of Belonging
>
> Support for the Community
>
> Developing Leadership Pipelines in Asia
>
> Supporting Workplace Flexibility

Employee Resource Groups – Creating Sources of Innovation and Community Connection

Employee Resource Groups (ERGs) continue to play an important role in supporting Asian Pacific American employees. In fact, ERGs are a key component of support for diversity for virtually all of the participating employers. Many organizations have found that aligning the ERGs with organizational strategies and goals has led to business success. Executive leadership sponsorship, mentoring programs offered through the ERG, and ERG-sponsored programs that are widely attended by all employees were approaches consistently mentioned by Finalist companies.

Cardinal Health views their commitment to Asian Pacific American employees as an ongoing obligation – not a onetime event. APAN, Cardinal Health's Employee Resource Group, strives to be better each year by doing more for its membership and the community. Cardinal Health continues to serve as a lead sponsor for the Columbus Asian Festival, which is a two-day event with a mission to promote and preserve a rich Asian cultural heritage. The event showcases Asian fine arts and provides educational programs, resources, and services to Cardinal Health members, stakeholders, and the community at large. Cardinal Health provides health screenings at the event, and these continue to be a popular and valuable service, particularly for Asian Pacific Americans. Many organizations such as **3M** and **Cisco** find that multiple APA groups are needed to help fully support their employee population. Cisco actually has three executive sponsored groups that focus on Asian Pacific American employees: one focused on countries in the Pacific Rim, one focused on Indian culture, and one focusing on Muslim interests.

One trend that continues is transitioning ERGs from affiliation groups toward groups that align with organizational values. For example, **PepsiCo** has shifted the focus of their Employee Resource Group from providing social support and networking to making substantial contributions to the company's strategy. "In the old days, ERGs were the diversity and inclusion programs. Today we've been able to unleash them to do what we can to add value," said Maurice Cox, Vice President, Corporate Development & Diversity. These groups allow APA employees to have a voice, to be connected and unified. But they also provide an avenue for all employees to learn from each other by bringing people from all backgrounds together to share in cultural events. Every employee is encouraged

> Employee networks have been the most effective programs by far for supporting the Asian Pacific American employee.
>
> – Survey respondent

to be part of the events and programs planned by the ERGs.

To ensure the success of this new strategic alignment, sponsorship from the top is critical. For example, at **New York Life,** every ERG has at least one executive team sponsor who provides guidance and execution of programming. At **3M,** executive sponsors meet with ERG chairs regularly – usually monthly or quarterly – to provide coaching and feedback on making the ERG strategy more business relevant. The ERG becomes a built-in think tank providing insight into market segments and product branding.

 **GE** has found the best way to support its Affinity Networks through a combination of centralized executive sponsorship and local chapter participation. Their Asian Pacific American Forum (APAF) has 17 hubs and 28 chapters nationally for the 9000+ APA employees across the U.S. APAF is led by its three national champions and sponsored by two Senior Vice Presidents on the Chairman's senior management staff. APAF's national leaders, and those of the other affinity forums at GE, attend quarterly meetings with the Chairman, their Senior VP sponsors, and the Corporate Diversity Council led by Deborah Elam, VP, Chief Diversity Officer for GE. In 2010, APAF held over 250 events, including training workshops, networking sessions, speaker events, talent roundtables, community service events, and cultural celebrations. In each of the past two years, APAF's sponsors and national champions have visited regional hubs across the US, meeting over 3,300 employees. The events included business overviews, leadership panels and roundtables, external speakers, and government guests, as well as training workshops and growth leadership awards.

TimeWarner In many organizations, ERGs provide critical input in understanding the Asian marketplace. As a content company, **Time Warner** is continuously striving to reach diverse audiences, not just in the US but around the world. Time Warner's comprehensive inclusion efforts are designed to target each group within the organization. By regularly soliciting their employees' input and feedback on content, content providers like HBO and Warner Bros. help employees see their contribution to the company's success and help the company reach their growing diverse audience. For example, Warner Bros. often holds focus groups on the studio lot and asks its ERGs to participate. "It is a great way for our employees to feel connected to our company, and also really shapes the outcome of a product (and makes it better!)." Leveraging ERGs in this way provides APAs with increased impact and visibility within the organization while improving the applicability of the products.

Career Development for APA Employees – Keeping High-Potentials in the Pipeline Through Career-Pathing and Coaching

Many organizations we talked with discussed ways in which leadership training, and training provided for high potential employees, is tailored to APA employees. Targeted training often includes helping APAs navigate the corporate culture. Understanding the importance of "personal branding," assertiveness, and promoting one's own career/accomplishments was often mentioned.

At **Colgate-Palmolive**, leadership development is conducted for "early-in-career" high potentials by senior executives through their Colgate Leadership Challenge program. Through this program, high potentials are able to take part in action learning teams where they analyze important business issues and identify resolutions. Training and development at Colgate-Palmolive has several programs that focus on the unique circumstances of APA employees and other minority populations. Programs like this provide increased visibility for talented employees regardless of ethnic background. Facilitating identification of key talent based on objective measurement of potential (rather than traditional networking) provides APAs with increased opportunities for visibility and career development.

PepsiCo's APA employees give the company high marks for the visibility of APA leaders within the company. Although it certainly sets the stage to have an Indian as CEO (Indian-born Indra Nooyi has served as PepsiCo's CEO since 2006), PepsiCo's diversity team will tell you "she is just one person." Talent sustainability is a core part of PepsiCo's corporate directive. The goal of their Performance with a Purpose directive is to provide people with rich job and development experiences throughout their careers with the company.

Coaching plays a big part of employee development as well as building an open and inclusive culture at **Kraft Foods.** They are in year two of their formal peer coaching program, which focuses on the professional development of women and people of color. The objective of this initiative is to increase these employees' effectiveness in their current assignments, increase their effectiveness in anticipated future assignments, and advise managers as they coach and develop high-potential women and people of color. The uniqueness of the program involves engaging a diverse group of internal coaches (current directors and Vice Presidents) to provide developmental support to women, professionals of color, and managers, ensuring that professional development plan objectives are achieved or exceeded.

Many companies have found that commitment to promoting a diverse workplace is a key to business success. **Kaiser Permanente** knows that the communities they serve are made up of very diverse populations, so their continued success is dependent upon providing culturally competent medical care to these communities, which is aided through the development of employees from various backgrounds. To ensure such development, Kaiser Permanente has developed a Diversity Leadership Development program to enable the identification of high potentials from diverse backgrounds.

KPMG has a track record not only of supporting APAs in their career growth efforts, but of promoting APAs into leadership roles. In fact, in 2010, 18.2% of those promoted to manager level or above at KPMG self-identified as Asian/Pacific Islanders. Diversity among their leaders is a business imperative for KPMG. Such diversity demonstrates a culture of inclusion that offers opportunities to all, helping ensure that the organization has the best people as well as a team that reflects a rich mix of backgrounds, experiences, and perspectives. They believe this mix generates better ideas, creates more effective leaders, and builds stronger relationships with diverse clients and communities. Much of their success in building careers may be attributed to the emphasis that is put on career growth throughout the firm. Training offered is extensive, career exploration support is widely available and supported by leadership, and more than 12,000 employees and partners (more than 60% of the population) participate in formal mentoring programs. Rotational assignments are also key to career development at KPMG, strengthening a culture that truly fosters learning. At KPMG, people work as a team and therefore are very willing to help peers and colleagues learn. The environment strongly promotes a sense of communication, teamwork, and collaboration.

Cisco understands that innovation is driven by diversity. Cisco's culture supports hard work and innovation. Many APA employees find that their core values support the company culture, in which people are rewarded for working hard and working smart. Nearly one-third of their organization is composed of engineers, and nearly 80% of those engineers are of Asian descent. As a result, the company culture is heavily influenced by APA culture.

As an organization that hires many scientists and engineers, *3M* works hard to ensure that employees have opportunities for career growth throughout their careers. To ensure that scientists do not get "pigeonholed" into a specific technical field, the company has carefully planned career discussions built into its appraisal process. For all technical roles, there are two career paths available: a technical path and a managerial path. Discussion about those career path options are included in performance management discussions, and employees can shift from one path to another at any point in their careers if opportunities are available.

At **Pfizer**, leadership development for APAs is enhanced by a partnership with Leadership Education for Asian Pacifics (LEAP), an organization that provides customized leadership development tailored to APAs, created by APAs. LEAP

provides development for all types of business sectors, including education, nonprofit, private, and public.

Creating a Sense of Belonging – Valuing Differences, Not "Fixing" a Problem

Finalists acknowledged that the learning goes both ways. As companies embrace diversity, that diversity contributes to the corporate culture, and the culture begins to change in new and different ways.

At **PG&E**, diversity and inclusion are important parts of the organizational culture, as many ERGs have been in place for 25 years or more. Each year, the company holds annual diversity celebrations that include talent performances by the employees, and awards are given to "Diversity Champions" by the president of the company.

Freddie Mac ensures that all employees understand the company's commitment to diversity, inclusion, and engagement by introducing them to all of the ERGs during their first week of employment. In addition, new hires meet with an ambassador one-on-one to help the employee navigate his/her way through the organization. These practices have increased retention at Freddie Mac.

For example, according to some, one challenge facing employees of Asian descent is a tendency toward a less assertive communication style. In many organizations, a lack of assertiveness may result in fewer promotions, lower wages, or fewer opportunities for career growth. To counter this, many organizations have programs in place that help APA employees be more assertive, including workshops, support groups, and mentoring programs to bring APA employees "out of their shell," so to speak. Freddie Mac is well aware of some of these potential issues, so they have brought in prominent Asian American speakers such as Jane Hyun (author – *Breaking the Bamboo Ceiling*), Norman Mineta, former U.S. Secretary of Transportation and Commerce, and Tammy Duckworth, Assistant Secretary of the U.S. Department of Veterans Affairs. These types of speaker series have helped educate leaders and executive management about the unique challenges to the APA community and promoted the advancement of APA employees.

Because of PANG (Pan Asian Network Group) at **Sodexo,** many employees of Asian descent stated they "felt they finally belonged" at the company. APA employees have stated that they've gained visibility in the workplace through various PANG initiatives such as webinars, networking, workshops, and volunteering. One Sodexo employee stated, "Since I started to accept and embrace my own culture, I no longer felt embarrassed when I didn't pronounce some words right due to my accent or use proper grammar. I feel like I am becoming more comfortable."

To ensure a sense of belonging for all employees, **Lear** employs a culture of "no bullies." The culture of respect starts at the top and is very strong. The CEO himself talks about it a lot and takes it very seriously, knowing thousands of Lear employees by name. The result is – a very friendly company that feels like a family. And bullies? Well, they're simply not "invited back" to work.

Pfizer doesn't believe it is enough to say "this is America, get with the program." They not only help APA employees in showcasing their strengths, but also focus on training others (particularly managers) to appreciate and utilize the unique cultural differences that exist throughout the company.

At **McDonald's** the focus is all about leveraging those individual differences. Rather than trying to train employees to overcome perceived shortcomings related to cultural differences, the message is "we want you to come to work the way you are. Don't make an effort

McDonald's in Hacienda, California saw a rise in customer counts after bringing in a Feng Shui master to help with remodeling plans.

to change yourself, but rather use your cultural characteristics and unique gifts to be successful." At McDonald's, developing an inclusive environment means valuing others for what they are and creating incentives for being curious about other cultures.

This knowledge and appreciation of different cultures has provided invaluable insights and has allowed McDonald's to be nimble in serving their diverse customer base. As McDonald's sought to have a bigger impact on APAs both internally and externally, a team of franchisees, employees, and suppliers developed the McDonald's Asian Vision. This gave the company deeper insights into Asian tastes, cultures, and other relevant information. In one case, as a result of this work, one of McDonalds' non-Asian franchisees who had a large Asian consumer base brought in a Feng Shui master when his restaurant was being rebuilt. His customer counts increased, as did profits.

Employee Resource Groups can help in creating inclusive environments by building cultural understanding and respect. For example, at **Colgate-Palmolive**, the Asian Action Network (AAN) featured a Country Series on India, Thailand, and the Philippines. The group celebrated social/cultural events that included Lunar New Year, Diwali, film screenings, tea tasting, a Ping-Pong summer social, and artists. AAN recently hosted sessions on "Emerging

Market Innovation" and "Growth Opportunities in the Asian-American Market Segment."

Colgate-Palmolive employees celebrate Lunar New Year at their headquarters in New York City.

Support for the Community – Going Beyond Festival Celebrations to Create Value-Added and Business-Relevant Community Relationships

For many APA employees, support for family goes beyond being available for the 3rd grade play at school. Because of traditional values held by many APA employees, family focus includes not just care for children but also for parents or grandparents. At **McDonald's,** flexibility and support for family is important to the company as well. Family is a key part of the work environment and built into formal and informal work-related activities. Not only do work-related parties include families, but employees bring their children to work, and families of employees become extended families of the company. The company has even coined the term "McFamily." An example of that can be found in the fact that many of their owner operators are second and third generations of previous and current owner operators. Being aware of family values has helped McDonald's maintain a strong employee base and strong

connections with communities. McDonald's employees support local, national, and global APA organizations through dedicating their time and skills, and they support events in the community such as the Tet Festival in Los Angeles, the Lunar New Year Parade in San Francisco, and the Cherry Blossom Festival in Washington, DC, which help to create positive change in the communities in which employees live and work.

PG&E, through their APA ERG, InspirAsian, supports the needs of APA employees and families by hosting brown bag lunch sessions on referral services for elder care. They actively support a local group called Self-Help for the Elderly, which was started over 40 years ago in the Chinatown neighborhood of San Francisco and serves 25,000 senior citizens per year. InspirAsian partners with the community to host cultural events such as the Lunar New Year Festival, the Cherry Blossom Festival, the Tet Festival, and the Moon Festival. Employees are highly engaged in the process throughout the planning and execution of these events.

Many companies have chosen to establish partnerships with community organizations that promote the success of youth.

In its focus on community service, one shining example of **GE's** APAF contributions is its "Igniting Minds" initiative. Looking to make a difference in the U.S.'s educational crisis in math and

Maryam Hameed, a member of GE's Asian Pacific American Forum, assists Milwaukee middle schoolers with math through GE's "Igniting Minds"

science, APAF leveraged the strengths of the forum to find a way to help improve math and science scores of America's youth. With the help of the National Council of Teachers of Mathematics, APAF developed a program model and curriculum designed to help teach math fundamentals. The program has piloted at six schools, with more on the horizon. The participating schools have loved this volunteer program, which is taught by GE employees in a fun, real-life application activity in the classroom. Feedback from school administrators, teachers, students, and parents has been uniformly enthusiastic, at a time when government cutbacks in tutoring have been substantial.

3M also looks for ways to share the strengths of their techno-savvy employees with the community. As part of its Visiting Wizard program, 3M partners with specific schools to get kids excited about science. The Visiting Wizards bring science to life with interesting demonstrations and hands-on experiments. Any 3M employee – not just technical staff – can volunteer for the program. If you're not a scientist, no problem; 3M trains the volunteers to know what they need to lead the program.

3M Visiting Wizard and Senior Process Engineer Donald Alston demonstrates principles of cryogenics to a group of children attending Rondo Days in St. Paul, MN.

Kaiser Permanente has also established a partnership with INROADS, an organization that is committed to providing professional opportunities and programs for underprivileged and minority populations. Programming involves placing students at organizations during the summers as interns, with the goal of having each student hired upon graduation.

New York Life's Asian Network Group has partnered with two organizations: APEX and SAYA, which provide children with one-on-one relationships with caring adults who can serve as positive role models. These types of initiatives can help underprivileged individuals become highly successful in the workforce.

Support for the community often extends to supporting employees who support the community. *3M's* community support efforts are extensive, creating a partnership between employee and employer to support the community. Any 3M employee, current or retired, can volunteer up to 40 hours of their time, and 3M will match with a cash contribution to eligible nonprofits. Other organizations such as *Goldman Sachs*, *New York Life*, and *Time Warner* provide for employees to take paid time from work for volunteer activities, because they want their employees to have the time to engage in meaningful volunteer experiences in their communities. Empowering APA employees to make decisions about what charities they will support helps ensure that community support will be relevant to employees and more meaningful to the larger community.

Community TeamWorks, *Goldman Sachs'* signature volunteer program, allows people time away from work each year to volunteer on a team- **Goldman Sachs** based project with a nonprofit organization. In 2010, 45 Goldman Sachs offices partnered with 895 nonprofit community partners worldwide. More than 25,300 Goldman Sachs people joined with family and friends to contribute over 148,800 hours to the communities where they work and live. Examples of nonprofits or charities Goldman Sachs supports include the Coalition of Asian Pacific Americans, the Millennium High School, Working Playground: MS 131 Chinatown Transformation Project, the American Cancer Society's A Taste of Asia event, Japanese American Social Services, and the Asian Professional Extension, Inc.

CORNING Members of one of *Corning's* APA ERGs, Corning Chinese Association (CCA), have strong support from executive leadership and are relied upon to develop business solutions. They are even called upon to provide assistance in areas outside of core business needs. The Corning Museum of Glass, which is affiliated with Corning, had a unique problem that members of CCA were well equipped to handle. The museum employees were having a hard time with some of the cultural differences in shopping they saw with Asian tourists. Patrons would often open packaging and attempt to negotiate pricing. Members of CCA were able to provide insight, and provided the museum with concrete and actionable recommendations, such as using better signage and implementing clear communications on bartering – as well as recommendations on crowd flow and customer service approaches, and a suggestion to hire more Asians as clerks and guides. Members of CCA found this experience useful in developing their coaching/mentoring skills and learning how to act in those capacities.

Cardinal Health has recently strengthened its ties with Asia by acquiring a company in China. Cardinal Health CEO George Barrett had laid out a plan for the China market and the strategy for getting there at one of the company's "Lunch & Learns." When the Chinese company was purchased, Cardinal Health leadership knew they had the support of their employee resource group (APAN) behind them. At a subsequent "Lunch & Learn", the President of Cardinal Health China, Erik Zwisler, helped build a bridge between those on the ground in China and those in the U.S.

Developing Leadership Pipelines in Asia – Leveraging Critical APA Insights

Global assignments are a key part of the employee growth and advancement programs at **KPMG**. Through their Global Mobility program, professionals are provided an opportunity to take temporary assignments in KPMG international

Andrew Lau, a Tax Manager from KPMG's New York Office, goes for a ride in Vietnam while on a Global Mobility assignment.

member firms around the world. Currently, more than 104 professionals from the KPMG U.S. member firm are on temporary assignments at KPMG member firms in the Asia/Pacific region. This represents about 37% of the participants in the program.

At **Corning**, there has been an increased corporate focus on developing leadership pipelines in Asia. Corning has added to their Global Emerging Leaders (GEL) program to create a more targeted program that works to develop leaders within specific regions. This program – Regional Emerging Leaders (REL) – pulls from cultural needs unique to the targeted regions and provides tailored training for the most relevant business and developmental needs. Corning expects that as a result of this focus, they will be faster to market, be quicker at gathering and interpreting market intelligence effectively, and improve their relationships with the government and with non-governmental organizations (NGOs).

Pfizer believes in exhibiting inclusive behaviors and demonstrating respect for the individual in everything that they do worldwide. Overall, the company is committed to being a great place to work for all colleagues, which also means paying attention to specific needs of their diverse colleague base. The company supplements management and leadership development programs by leveraging its colleague resource group, the Asian Pacific American Colleague Resource Group (APAG), to assess and identify internal and external resources for Asians' professional development. As an example, a few APAG chapters have engaged Leadership Education for Asian Pacifics (LEAP) to deliver customized training. They have sent senior Asian leaders to participate in the executive leadership development program at Stanford School of Management, which recently launched a program specifically designed for APAs. APAG has developed what it hopes will be a novel and innovative mentoring program that increases the visibility of rising APA leaders.

In addition, Pfizer supports APA employees in showcasing their strengths and utilizing unique cultural differences that exist throughout the company to support their businesses. Pfizer has seen momentum and growth in the APAG. The group receives strong leadership support and has positioned itself to be able to provide critical insights that will help drive Pfizer businesses forward in key emerging markets in Asia.

Goldman Sachs views the BRICs (Brazil, Russia, India, and China) and other growth markets as among the most significant opportunities for their global franchise. Over the last few years, Goldman Sachs has generated roughly 20% of their revenues from Asia. The firm's success in growth markets has been contingent upon its ability to work effectively across cultures and attract, develop, and retain strong talent. A few examples of initiatives that

have proved to strengthen the engagement and retention of Asian professionals and increase awareness include *Doors Wide Open,* a program designed to educate the U.S. population on the firm's activities in Asia and encourage professionals to pursue opportunities in the region; and the *Loft Series*, which serves as a forum for Asian women to engage in candid and informal conversation with senior leaders about career development and advancement at the firm, specifically as it relates to multicultural women.

As a supplier to the auto industry, **Lear** sees understanding emerging markets in Asia as fundamental to their future growth. That's why learning about global business is so important to the company. Expatriate assignments are a key part of their leadership training. Lear finds that it's important to provide employees with the opportunity to learn in a global environment. In many cases that means support not just for employees but for their families as well. In fact, more than 1000 Lear employees work outside their home country – that's 10% of their workforce. That number includes about 300 full-scale relocations, including families; 300 employees on short-term assignments for up to one year; and 400 employees who split their time – three weeks in, three weeks out. To maximize success in these assignments, Lear places employees in a community where they have the support they need from other expatriates.

At **3M**, the percentage of APA leaders is above average, due to practices that involve recognizing leaders who promote diversity and inclusion, and making APAs more visible through mentorship programs. Because of 3M's large business presence in the Asia Pacific region, having so many APA leaders is helpful to the company, as they provide further insight into APA markets, suppliers, and customers. In addition, when Asian Pacific leaders visit the company's headquarters in St. Paul, the company's APA leaders host them in order to provide U.S. business insights, thus strengthening the ties between the two regions.

Time Warner, like many organizations, feels it's important to align their philanthropic giving with their company values and "who we are as a company." At Time Warner, they're all about telling stories, and therefore much of their philanthropy focuses on the importance and value of supporting a diversity of voices. Partnering with Asia Society and Indian film schools, they invite up to 10 filmmakers per year to create innovative film projects in India.

Supporting Workplace Flexibility – APA Issues Are Not Always "Diversity" Issues

KPMG offers many types of alternative work arrangements that include flexibility in schedules, locations, and hours worked in order to help employees better manage their personal lives while meeting professional commitments – and the firm finds that the employees highly value these programs. At the same time, the firm supports "informal" arrangements for employees who need flexibility for a day or two to deal with a temporary issue. The firm even offers a sabbatical program providing opportunities for employees to apply for 4 to 12 week sabbaticals. Participating employees are compensated at 20% of their regular salary. More than 1,200 employees have taken or plan to take a sabbatical through this program, which has been in place since 2009. The key to its success is the positive attitude from leadership, who considers sabbaticals an important element of the firm's flexibility package and is supportive of employees who use the program. When employees return to KPMG from sabbaticals, they are often refreshed and full of new ideas. They bring a renewed sense of purpose and creativity back to their work, with excellent results for both themselves and the firm.

At **Sodexo,** employees are given more control over their work arrangements through an initiative called "Flexibility Works!" Work is focused on the outcomes and results, and employees are able to determine where, when, and how they will get the work done. Employees report more engagement and ability to produce better results as an outcome. At **Kraft Foods**, flexibility is so important that a few years ago they added a Director of Workplace Flexibility. The corporation is currently converting to an open space environment where many corporate employees, and their managers, are truly free to work how and where they like. Rather than being assigned to cubicles and computers, employees choose their own workspace, are reimbursed for the computer and phone that they choose, and are encouraged to develop the work schedule that works best for them. Offices and cubicles have been replaced with team areas, which may include couches, chairs, exercise equipment, booths, and tables. Leveraging the latest and most effective technologies, they meet Kraft Foods' business needs as well as their personal needs. To facilitate collaboration, teams establish core work days where employees work in the office. On other days employees are free to work where and how they are most effective. Managers and employees have reported improved productivity and more time to dedicate to their work-life concerns. While this innovative flexibility initiative is not by any means exhaustive, it is one that Kraft Foods and their employees are very excited about!

Summary

Finalists have several unique practices that set them apart as best places to work for Asian Pacific Americans. Most companies have innovative scheduling practices that allow for employees to work where, when, and how they wish, which is highly supportive of families. In addition, many companies support family and community through providing paid time off for volunteering activities such as mentoring and environmental improvement. Initiatives like these make a company a great place to work for members of all cultures.

However, finalists have gone above and beyond with specific initiatives and programming aimed at promoting Asian Pacific American employees into leadership positions. At most of our participating companies, employee resource groups have taken on initiatives that celebrate Asian Pacific Americans through creating a sense of belonging, and providing them with resources such as workshops that can help them succeed both at work and at home. Sponsorship from the top is common in these companies, which allow the company's commitment to diversity to trickle down into the company culture. Many of the finalists indicated that they have a strong presence at many annual Asian festivals, such as Lunar New Year, Diwali, Tet, and city-specific events such as the Cherry Blossom Festival and the Columbus Asian Festival, but they go beyond simple presence to developing strategic relationships within the community.

Many of the finalists also indicated that they have specific career development programs tailored to Asian Pacific Americans. Some of these programs have included networking and communication skills, while others focused on developing a diverse set of high potentials in order to promote diversity in senior leadership. In addition, many companies put the focus on celebrating the knowledge and expertise brought to them by their APA employees, which has led to increased profits for many companies. Some companies have even taken these practices a step further, by pursuing business ventures in Asia. Many finalists note that the expertise of their APA employee base is imperative for fully understanding the dynamics of the Asian market. Many of these companies expect to see growth in Asia that will translate into greater profits and continued success of the company.

SURVEY DIMENSION FINDINGS

Dimension Summary – Growth and Leadership continue to lag

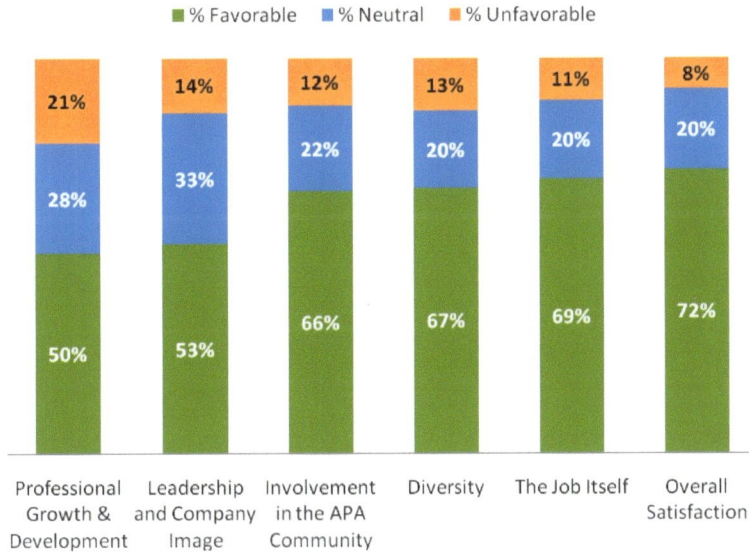

Legend: ■ % Favorable ■ % Neutral ■ % Unfavorable

Dimension	% Favorable	% Neutral	% Unfavorable
Professional Growth & Development	50%	28%	21%
Leadership and Company Image	53%	33%	14%
Involvement in the APA Community	66%	22%	12%
Diversity	67%	20%	13%
The Job Itself	69%	20%	11%
Overall Satisfaction	72%	20%	8%

Asian Pacific American employees provided high ratings for *overall satisfaction* with their employer, with 72% favorable responses for questions in this dimension. *Involvement in the APA community*, *diversity*, and the *job itself* also received high ratings from APA employees. APA employees gave lower ratings to items related to *professional growth & development* and to *leadership and company image*. Detailed results for each dimension point to key areas of opportunity and are highlighted in the following sections.

Overall Satisfaction: A perception of not belonging persists

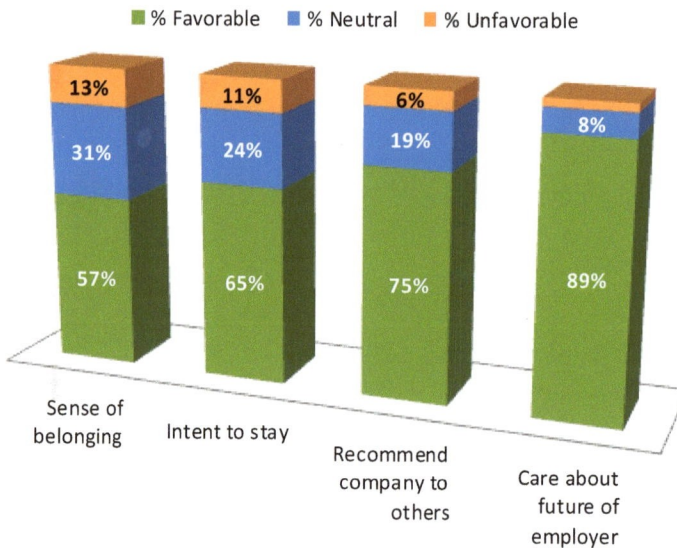

Legend: ■ % Favorable ■ % Neutral ■ % Unfavorable

Sense of belonging: 57% Favorable, 31% Neutral, 13% Unfavorable
Intent to stay: 65% Favorable, 24% Neutral, 11% Unfavorable
Recommend company to others: 75% Favorable, 19% Neutral, 6% Unfavorable
Care about future of employer: 89% Favorable, 8% Neutral

For the second year in a row, results indicate that Asian Pacific American employees are *highly engaged* and *committed to the success* of their company. Eighty-nine percent (89%) of employees included in our study report they *really care about the future of their company*, 65% say they would *remain with their employer* if offered a comparable job elsewhere, and three-fourths say they would *recommend their employer* to other Asian Pacific Americans as a good place to work. While they are committed to the organization, APAs do not always feel a *sense of belonging* at the organization, with just over half (57%) of respondents feeling they belong.

Improving a sense of belonging for Asian Pacific American employees, as well as strengthening connections with co-workers can help increase engagement levels for this group. Employee resource groups tailored to APAs, as well as providing ample networking opportunities, may help increase feelings of belonging.

The Job Itself: APA employees rewarded for skills and performance but want opportunities to demonstrate full potential

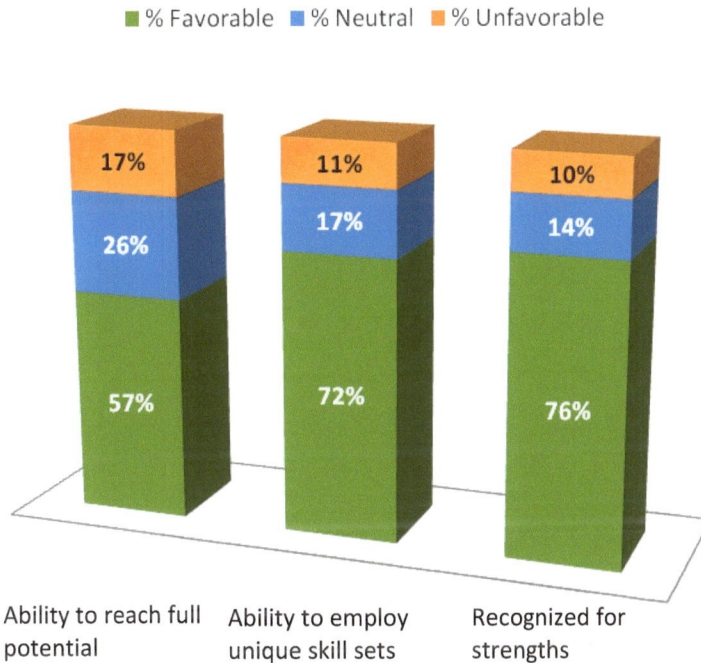

■ % Favorable ■ % Neutral ■ % Unfavorable

Most APA employees feel good about the jobs they hold and their ability to use their skills at work. Seventy-six percent (76%) reported that they were *recognized for individual strengths,* and 72% reported that they were able to employ *all of their skill sets at work.* Just over half (57%) of APAs reported that they were able to *reach their full potential* at their company, and more than one-quarter (26%) indicated that they were unsure.

These results relate to the perception of Asian Pacific American employees in key positions, including senior leadership positions. APAs are recognized for their skills and performance, yet desire opportunities to realize their full potential. Companies providing these opportunities, whether in leadership positions or in temporary assignments in Asia, positively impact employee engagement. It is important to identify the strengths of employees and to ensure that their work allows them to do what they do best every day – a practice that has been linked to increased employee engagement. Employees should be recognized for what they do well. Although this may seem like common sense, many APAs struggle with recognition of strengths other than those that many may associate with APAs. For other employees, their skills align with expectations for APAs, but then they feel pigeonholed – not given opportunities to build new skills outside what others may expect of APAs.

Diversity: Focus needed on promotion process and APA representation

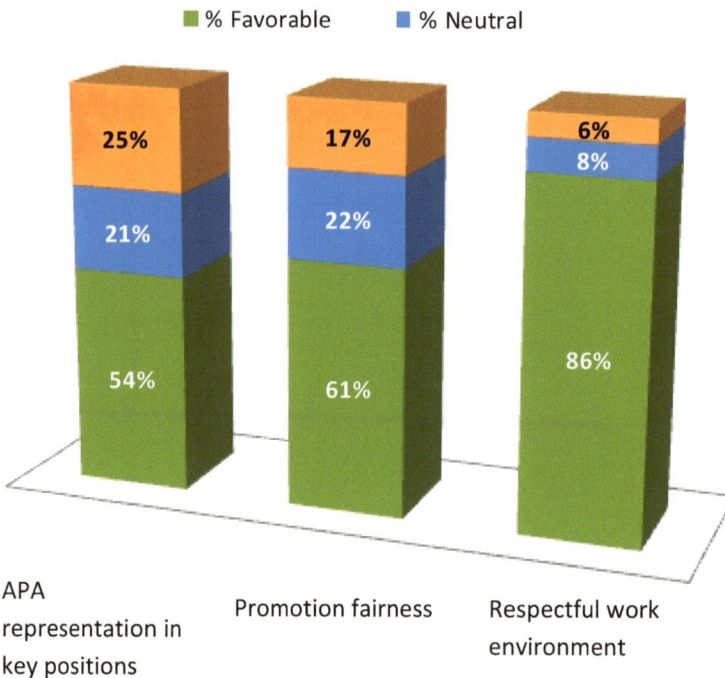

While Asian Pacific Americans give their companies' **commitment to diversity** high marks overall, specific items about fairness and support received lower ratings. Most respondents (86%) agree that their work environment is **respectful and free of offensive behavior**. Fewer feel positive about the implementation and/or impact of diversity efforts, with 61% of respondents agreeing that *promotions* are awarded to the *most deserving employees*. Lowest in this dimension is the perception of *representation of APAs in key positions*, with just over half (54%) of all employees finding the representation favorable.

Being in an engaging job provides employees with challenging work, a sense of personal achievement, and the opportunity to use skills and strengths. The perception that APAs may earn fewer promotions or have limited access to higher level jobs can be detrimental to engagement. Leadership programs tailored to APA employees, increased visibility to leadership through mentoring, and embracing differences in style and perspective are all strategies that companies may take to break down these perceived barriers to opportunity.

Professional Growth and Development: Leadership development is not enough

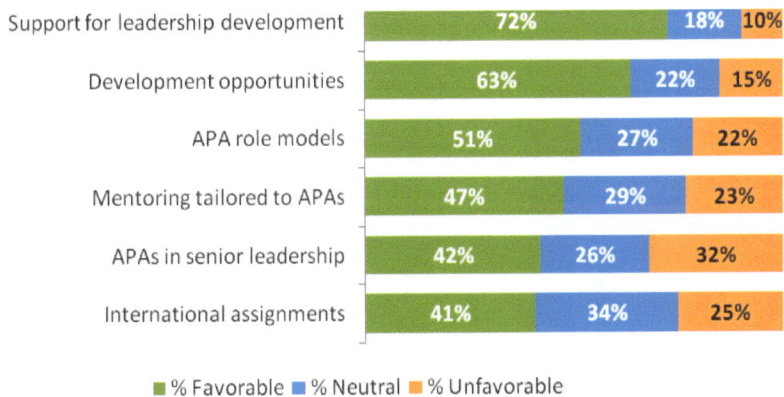

	% Favorable	% Neutral	% Unfavorable
Support for leadership development	72%	18%	10%
Development opportunities	63%	22%	15%
APA role models	51%	27%	22%
Mentoring tailored to APAs	47%	29%	23%
APAs in senior leadership	42%	26%	32%
International assignments	41%	34%	25%

■ % Favorable ■ % Neutral ■ % Unfavorable

Questions pertaining to *growth and development* received some of the lowest scores on the survey. Although most APA employees report that they *feel supported* in participating in leadership development activities (72%) and feel there are *opportunities for development* within their company (63%), far fewer employees (42%) see a *presence of APAs* in their company's current leadership team. About half of APA employees report that there are *APA role models* within their company (51%) or that their company offers *mentoring programs* tailored for APA employees (47%). Just

41% say that their employer encourages employees to pursue *international assignments in Asia*.

Representation in key positions demonstrates a clear commitment to diversity in action as well as words. It sends a clear signal to Asian Pacific American employees that they can become leaders of the company. To keep engagement up, it is important for companies to show a clear connection from development to achievement.

Involvement with APA Community: A company's internal APA community is what counts the most, and ERGs play an important role in driving engagement

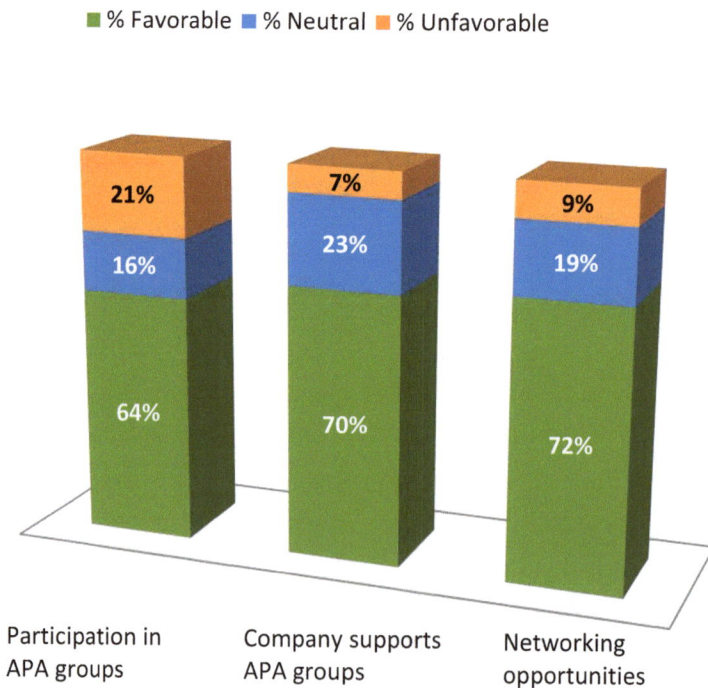

■ % Favorable ■ % Neutral ■ % Unfavorable

	Participation in APA groups	Company supports APA groups	Networking opportunities
% Unfavorable	21%	7%	9%
% Neutral	16%	23%	19%
% Favorable	64%	70%	72%

Employee resource groups (ERGs) continue to play an important role in supporting APAs within their work environments. Many APA employees feel good about their *opportunities to network* (72%) and the *support for APA employee resource groups* within their companies (70%). Approximately two-thirds (64%) of the APA employees in this study reported that they ***participate in APA resource groups*** supported by their employer.

Employee resource groups provide networking opportunities with peers and with APAs in other positions. ERG membership creates community within the organization by providing individuals with access to resources such as mentors and role models, so that Asian Pacific American employees have additional tools for growth and success.

Leadership and Company Image: While the importance of Asia itself is clear, perceptions of companies' efforts with APAs here at home is more mixed

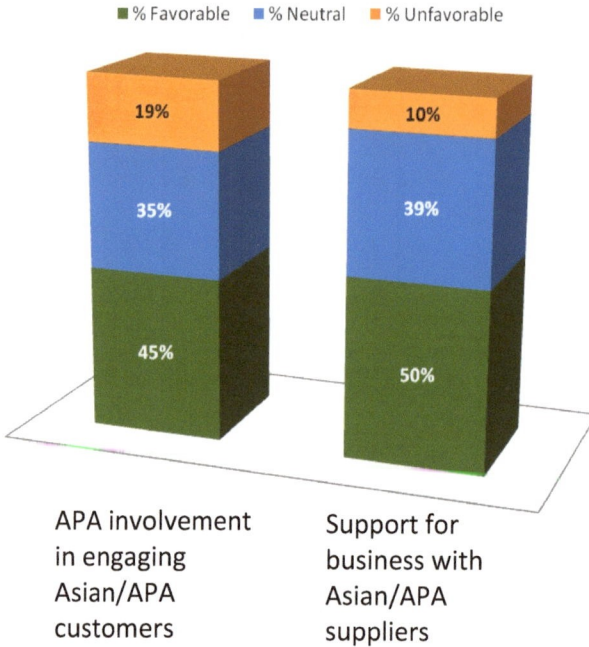

Survey results indicate a clear gap in APA perceptions around *leadership* and *company image*. The survey indicates that more than one-third of APA employees do not know whether their employers are drawing on Asian Pacific American employees to *engage Asian or APA customers* (35%) or whether their employers encourage and support doing *business with Asian Pacific American suppliers* (39%).

The growth in the economic importance of Asia means that all companies need to identify and leverage internal resources within their APA employees who can provide valuable insights into gaining market share. At the same time it is important to distinguish these from efforts to reach the APA market, in order to maximize growth both abroad in the Asia region and in the United States.

ANALYSIS OF TRENDS

Slight change in job tenure for survey respondents from 2010 to 2011

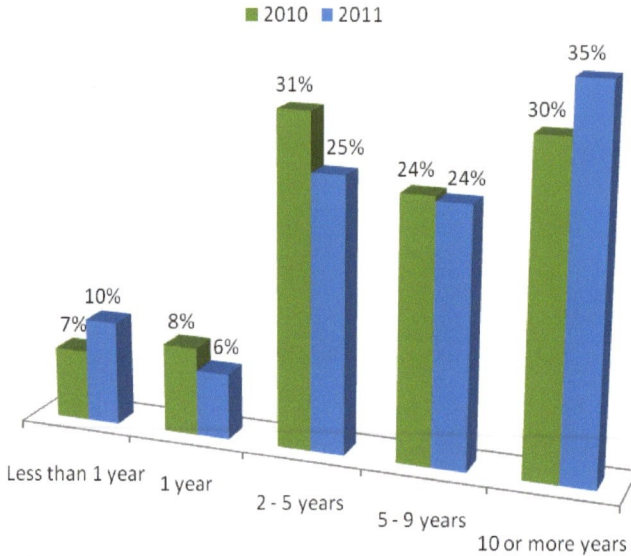

The makeup of respondents from last year to this stayed relatively the same in terms of age, gender, years in the US, heritage, and job level. One difference, however, was in job tenure. Slightly higher percentages of workers have spent *under a year in their job* and *over 10 years in their job*, whereas there is a slight decrease in the *2 to 5 year* category.

Several survey items showed increases in 2011, while only two scores decreased

Employee survey scores remained fairly stable compared with last year. There were a few areas that showed slight increases, including *opportunities for networking* with other APAs, *career development,* and presence of APAs in *senior leadership positions*. Only two *items showed decreases:* fewer employees feel their employers understand the *Asian marketplace*, and fewer feel *recognized for their strengths*.

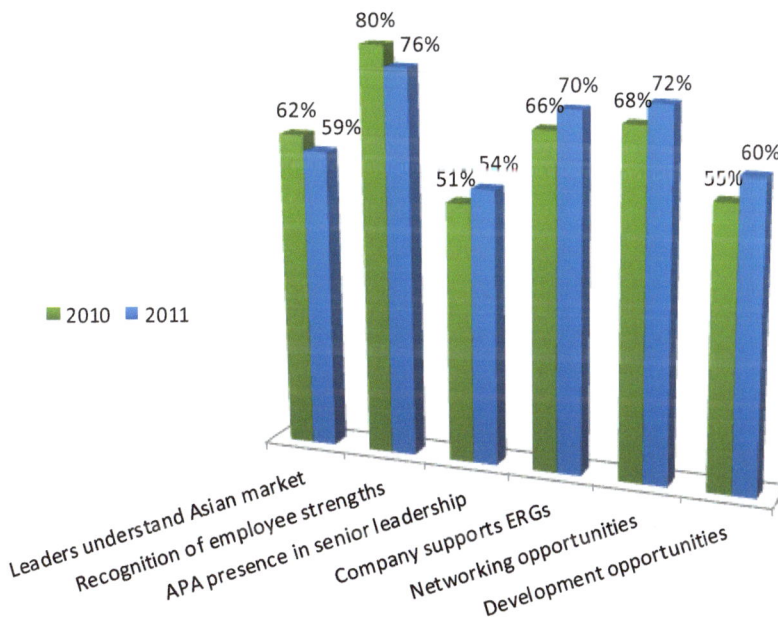

Bar chart comparing 2010 (green) and 2011 (blue) survey scores:

- Leaders understand Asian market: 62% (2010), 59% (2011)
- Recognition of employee strengths: 80% (2010), 76% (2011)
- APA presence in senior leadership: 51% (2010), 54% (2011)
- Company supports ERGs: 66% (2010), 70% (2011)
- Networking opportunities: 68% (2010), 72% (2011)
- Development opportunities: 55% (2010), 60% (2011)

Age Impacts

At career's start, APAs are more optimistic about development resources, recognition, and fair rewards

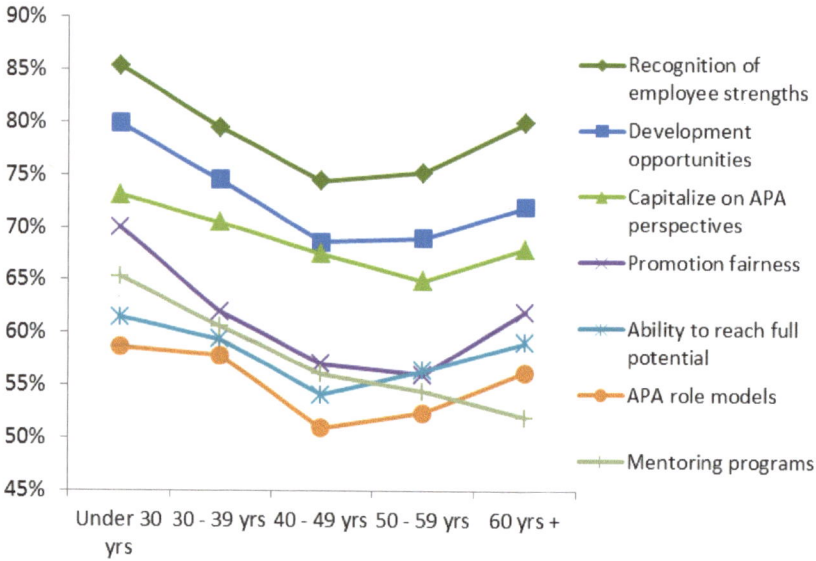

Younger APAs provide more positive feedback about support for **growth and career opportunities** within their company when compared with their more experienced colleagues. They tend to be more optimistic about opportunities for **career growth** and reaching their **full potential**. Younger employees are also more likely to believe that **promotions are based on merit,** and they respond more favorably to questions about **role models** and **mentoring**.

Closer to retirement, APAs are more vested in the company's future and have increased company loyalty

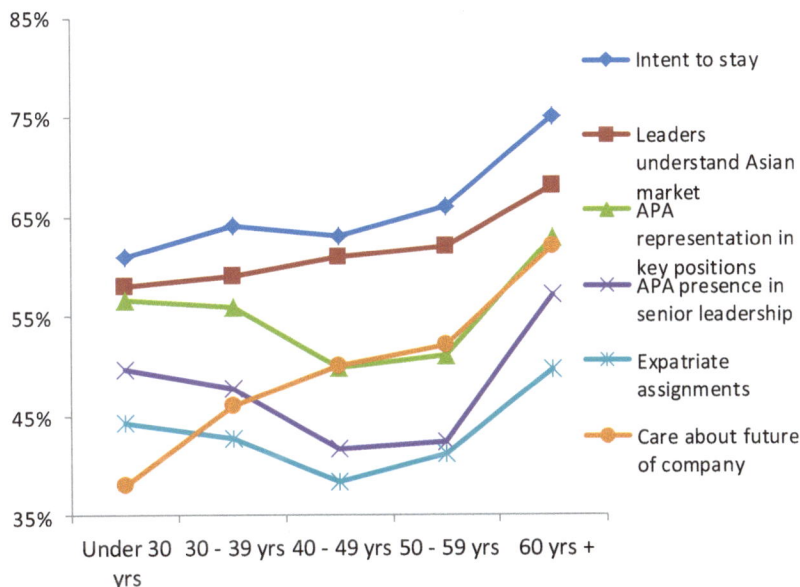

Older APAs were more likely to report that **APAs hold key positions** within their company and were more likely to report opportunities for **international assignments** in Asia. Older APAs also had increased **intentions to stay** with the company and agreed that they **care about the future of the company**.

Drivers of engagement influenced by age

Age also appears to influence employee drivers of engagement, especially in terms of their order of influence. In looking at the top five drivers for each age group, employees under 30 and over 50 have the same top five drivers, although the younger group values **development opportunities** more, whereas the older group values their companies' **commitment to diversity articulated in a mission statement.**

The middle age group shares some of the same engagement drivers as the younger and older groups. The accompanying chart shows the top five drivers, matched by color. To simplify comparison, the two drivers that apply only to the middle group – *recognition of strengths* and *promotion fairness* – are in black.

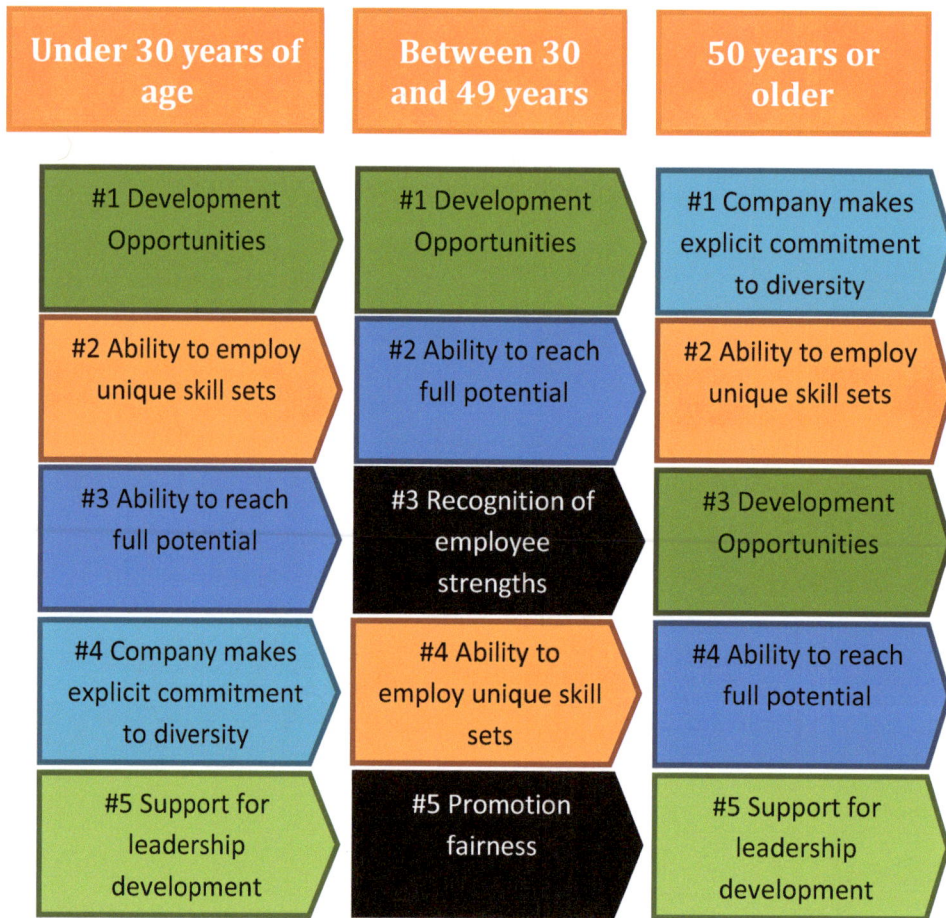

Under 30 years of age	Between 30 and 49 years	50 years or older
#1 Development Opportunities	#1 Development Opportunities	#1 Company makes explicit commitment to diversity
#2 Ability to employ unique skill sets	#2 Ability to reach full potential	#2 Ability to employ unique skill sets
#3 Ability to reach full potential	#3 Recognition of employee strengths	#3 Development Opportunities
#4 Company makes explicit commitment to diversity	#4 Ability to employ unique skill sets	#4 Ability to reach full potential
#5 Support for leadership development	#5 Promotion fairness	#5 Support for leadership development

The focus on rewards and recognition for the middle group could be due to where they are in their careers. In general, employees begin to make the move to management positions in these middle years. It becomes apparent to APA employees in this age group, that the perception of APAs as great executors but "not management material" could adversely affect their careers.

Gender Differences

Men had a tendency to provide slightly *higher ratings* of their work environment than did women in the study. The items with the largest differences are detailed below. Men provided more favorable ratings for items relating to *senior leadership* within the organization, *workgroup inclusion*, and *support for flexibility* in the work environment. The only item where women provided *higher scores* than men was whether the company offers *mentoring and/or sponsorship programs* for Asian Pacific American employees.

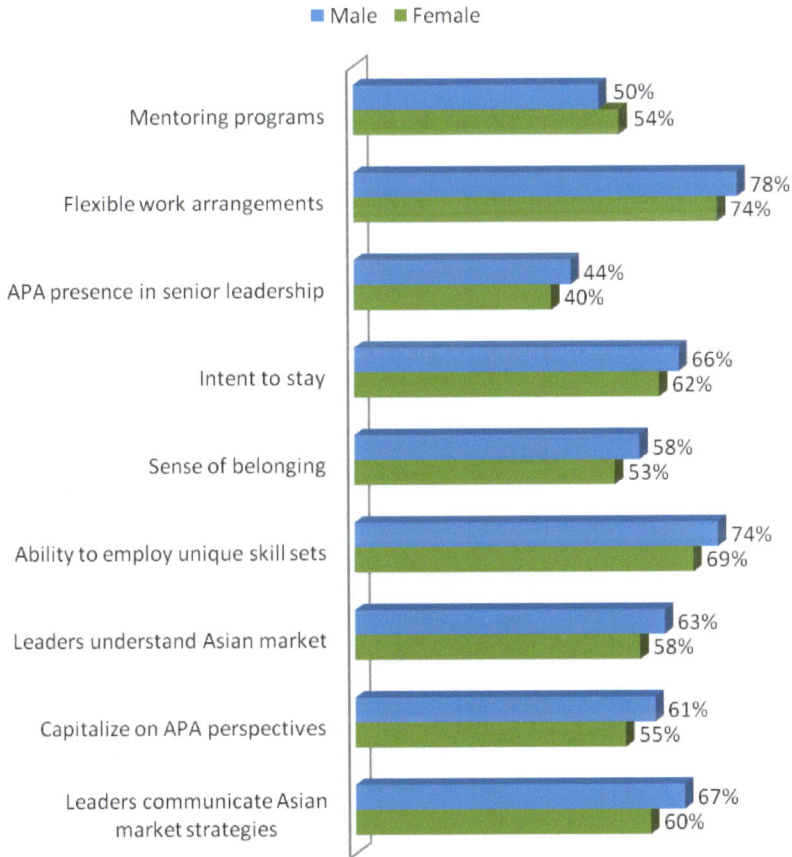

■ Male ■ Female

Item	Male	Female
Mentoring programs	50%	54%
Flexible work arrangements	78%	74%
APA presence in senior leadership	44%	40%
Intent to stay	66%	62%
Sense of belonging	58%	53%
Ability to employ unique skill sets	74%	69%
Leaders understand Asian market	63%	58%
Capitalize on APA perspectives	61%	55%
Leaders communicate Asian market strategies	67%	60%

Perspectives from LGBT Employees

Individuals identifying themselves as Lesbian, Gay, Bisexual, or Transgender (LGBT) were grouped to explore differences between these employees and other employees. Because of the low incidence of employees within the data (fewer than 3% of all employees in our sample), 2010 and 2011 data were merged for a more stable statistical analysis.

Overall, LGBT employees provided **lower scores on average for the following items**:

Please note: Due to the small numbers of LGBT employees responding to the survey, comparisons between LGBT APA and Other APA are anecdotal. A larger number of LGBT respondents is necessary to determine whether any differences are statistically significant.

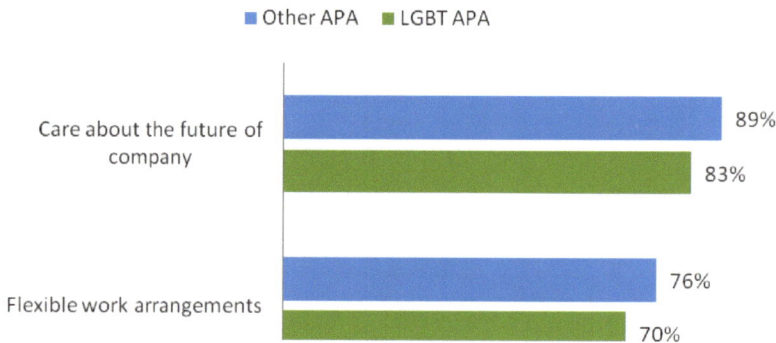

Other APA   LGBT APA

Care about the future of company	Other APA: 89%, LGBT APA: 83%
Flexible work arrangements	Other APA: 76%, LGBT APA: 70%

LBGT APA employees were **less likely to care** about the future of the company, and felt that their companies were **less supportive** of flexible work arrangements that help them meet their family and personal needs. However, these differences were only marginal and were not statistically different.

While LGBT employees were somewhat less likely to say the company supported **flexible work arrangements** that help meet family and personal commitments, they were more likely to report that their employers had *APA role models*. Items where LGBT employees were slightly more in agreement than other employees are listed below. Please note that only the first item on the list showed a difference that was statistically significant. Although some differences were large, reaching a level of statistical significance is difficult when sample sizes are small.

Please note: Because of small incidence rate and small sample size, most of the items below were not statistically significant.

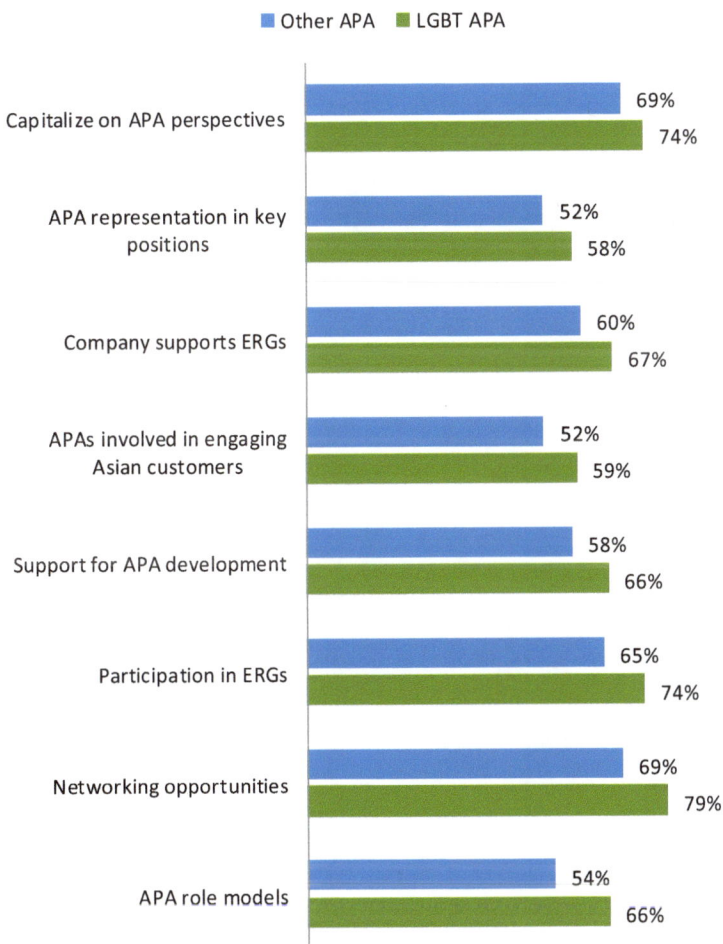

■ Other APA ■ LGBT APA

Item	Other APA	LGBT APA
Capitalize on APA perspectives	69%	74%
APA representation in key positions	52%	58%
Company supports ERGs	60%	67%
APAs involved in engaging Asian customers	52%	59%
Support for APA development	58%	66%
Participation in ERGs	65%	74%
Networking opportunities	69%	79%
APA role models	54%	66%

EMPLOYEE SUGGESTIONS

Employee Suggestions for Improving Practices Related to Asian Pacific Americans

Work-Life Effectiveness/Flexibility
- Allow time off for Asian holidays
- Have important literature available in common Asian languages
- Provide healthy Asian food choices in the cafeteria
- Provide employees flexibility to join interest groups outside the company

Improving Understanding of APA Culture
- Promote awareness through emails, especially during Asian Heritage Month
- Hold ethnic luncheons that create interest and awareness for different types of cuisine
- Offer rewards/discounts to employees who volunteer/participate in local cultural events
- Provide training around English words that have different meanings in different cultures
- Recruit non-APA employees to join APA employee resource groups

Helping APAs to Pursue Careers Working with Asian Customers
- Collaborate with rural areas in Asian countries for education opportunities
- Put an APA on all contracts with Asian customers
- Communicate the company's strategies for Asian markets to APA employees
- Develop an exchange program where employees can visit or work at affiliate offices in Asia

Increasing Feelings of Belonging & Opportunities to Network
- Have inter-company mingling events, especially with companies that have a large APA population

- Host corporate events at various satellite locations instead of the corporate office
- Allow APAs to have cross-country networking through conference calls or conferences

Diversity in Performance Management & Employee Development

- Develop a 1:1 mentoring program with matched ethnic backgrounds
- Recognize multi-language ability as an asset in performance management and utilize these skills in development
- Recognize the efforts of Diversity Councils during company-wide meetings
- Promote diversity within *all* teams of the company, such as sales and middle management

Creating or Sponsoring Programs Specific to Developing APA Employees

- Provide training/development around handling diverse internal/external customers
- Provide training/development around communicating with peers and superiors
- Allow APAs to visit local colleges/universities to recruit future APA employees

INTRODUCING THE AWARD RECIPIENTS

Introducing the Award Recipients

As part of the 2011 Asian Pacific Americans Corporate Survey, seven companies were recognized for providing inclusive workplaces that promote APAs to corporate leadership positions and draw on APA talent to grow their business at home and abroad. These seven were selected among the finalists for the quality of their APA programs as well as the results from their employee surveys. Awards were given for the following five categories:

- Overall Best Employer for Asian Pacific Americans
- Best Company for Asian Pacific Americans to Develop Workforce Skills
- Best Company in Promoting Asian Pacific Americans into Senior Leadership Positions
- Best Company for Support of the Asian Pacific American Community
- Best Company with the Most Innovative Practices

In addition to the Best Company awards, the Honor for Distinguished Practice award was also given to one company in each of the five categories.

Overall Best Employer for Asian Pacific Americans – KPMG

KPMG was specifically recognized for:

- A rich array of employee development, retention, and recruitment programs that positively impact APAs and all diverse employees along the entire leadership ladder
- Significant and deep senior-level commitment to Asian Pacific American organizations, including board and leadership positions for APA organizations; this speaks of a different level of commitment, not just dollars
- Broad-based opportunities for employees to get involved in supporting Asian community organizations, as evidenced by

the fact that 50 offices raised donations for Asian charities last year
- Global Mobility program – 37% of the participants are in Asian countries
- 60% of the population have mentors, and 18% of promotions to manager last year were to APAs
- A wide range of work-life effectiveness program options to fit different needs and circumstances

Honor for Distinguished Practice presented to *3M.*

Best Company for Asian Pacific Americans to Develop Workforce Skills – Colgate-Palmolive Company

Colgate-Palmolive was specifically recognized for:

- Identification and development of future leaders under a program conducted by senior executives
- A broad range of employee development programs, from work skills to global leadership
- Strong network groups that support company initiatives to attract, develop, and retain a diverse workforce, and that provide personal and professional development

Honor for Distinguished Practice presented to *McDonald's.*

Best Company in Promoting Asian Pacific Americans into Senior Leadership Positions – PepsiCo

PepsiCo was specifically recognized for:

- Two highly visible awards that recognize C-Suite employees whose leadership promotes diversity and inclusion
- Expanded leadership training
- Enlisting APAs to be more visible and involved through mentorship

All of which have caused the percentage of APAs on PepsiCo's corporate ladder to be above average.

Honor for Distinguished Practice presented to *3M.*

Best Company for Support of the Asian Pacific American Community – Cardinal Health

For the second year in a row, **Cardinal Health** was specifically recognized for:

- A breadth of programs instituted with global, national, and local Asian community organizations that were built with employee participation
- Numerous cross-cultural/cultural intelligence programs built by the company for the Asian community, including an external leadership development program
- Creation of cross-firm tools to enhance cultural understanding and individual and group cultural coaching

Honor for Distinguished Practice presented to *McDonald's.*

Best Company with the Most Innovative Practices – GE

This award, new in 2011, is based entirely on the descriptions of the innovative programs and initiatives that the company provides to its APA employees.

GE was specifically recognized for:

- Active involvement of senior officers in the company's corporate diversity council, which takes deep-dive looks into the diversity challenges and initiatives across all levels, businesses, and functions
- Strong support of the APA employee resource group, encouragement of members' outreach efforts, and internal surveys that have prompted new programs focused on APA issues and opportunities in the work environment
- Numerous programs to identify potential leaders early on and foster development of leadership skills
- Encouraging employees to help Asian communities in need across the globe
- Specific healthcare provider/education for issues that affect the APA population

Honor for Distinguished Practice presented to *KPMG.*

ASIA SOCIETY'S
GLOBAL LEADERSHIP INITIATIVES

Our Mission

To identify, inspire and develop leaders across the Asia-Pacific region, by convening leaders, creating networks, promoting new ideas, and sharing best practices across disciplines to catalyze informed discussion and address shared challenges.

For more than fifty years, Asia Society has been at the forefront of connecting Asians and Americans to foster strong partnerships in culture, business and global affairs. To that end, Asia Society believes that fostering leaders committed to working together to address shared challenges and realize common opportunities is the best investment we can make in the Asia-Pacific region's future. Over the past five years, Asia Society has launched four major new leadership initiatives - the Asia 21 Young Leaders Initiative, the Diversity Leadership Forum, the Women Leaders of New Asia Initiative, and a renewed Williamsburg policy leaders initiative. These exciting projects leverage Asia Society's unique role to foster leadership and catalyze collaboration.

Our Programs

ASIA 21 YOUNG LEADERS INITIATIVE

The quickening pace of global change presents new challenges that cross national boundaries; Asia and the United States must look to a new generation of leaders for fresh ideas and imaginative solutions. The Asia Society's Asia 21 Young Leaders Initiative is designed to identify, inspire and develop leaders across the Asia-Pacific community to build relationships, engage in transnational and interdisciplinary dialogue and cultural exchange, and develop cooperative responses for addressing shared challenges. Established in 2006, the Initiative now includes a network of over 700 young leaders representing every country in the region and all sectors, and has become the Asia-Pacific region's leading network for emerging leaders under the age of 40.

DIVERSITY LEADERSHIP FORUM

Established in 2009, the Diversity Leadership Forum provides a vital platform for corporations to discuss diversity and inclusion issues and best practices in regards to Asian professionals and analyze the influence of Diversity & Inclusion (D&I) on global market factors impacting businesses today. The 2012 Forum will take place on June 11, 2012.

The annual one-day conference includes, ground-breaking research results from Asia Society's annual Asian Pacific Americans Corporate Survey Report, an annual study that examines barriers to and best practices for career advancement of APAs, keynote and plenary session presentations featuring executives from global Fortune 1000 companies, and small group discussion tracks featuring relevant D&I topics and best practices.

The Forum attracts CEOs, CDOs, COOs, Asian ERG Leadership and Executive Advisors, Business Managers of Fortune 1000 companies and Diversity and Inclusion Managers, Educators and Consultants.

WILLIAMSBURG CONFERENCE

The Williamsburg Conference is the pre-eminent gathering of leading Americans and Asians committed to strengthening U.S.-Asia relations. Founded by John D. Rockefeller, 3rd in 1971, the Williamsburg Conference has brought top leaders from Asia and the United States together to explore the greatest challenges facing the Asia-Pacific community and develop creative approaches for addressing them. In the past 39 years, the conference has been held in the United States, Indonesia, Japan, Hong Kong, Canada, Malaysia, Australia (1977 and 1991), Thailand, the Philippines, Singapore, South Korea, China, Vietnam, New Zealand, India, Cambodia, and Mongolia.

WOMEN LEADERS OF NEW ASIA

As women enter the Asian work force in large numbers and step into leadership positions at institutions across the public and private sectors, there is a growing need for new forums to explore the important role of women leadership in Asia. Few professional networks of Asia-Pacific women currently exist to explore and address these issues. To address this gap, Asia Society has launched the Women Leaders of New Asia (WLNA) initiative which is fast becoming the premier cross-sector women's leadership network in the Asia Pacific region.

The Summit fosters discussion around a new paradigm of leadership that recognizes the contribution that women leaders in Asia can make. As Asia's global influence in the political, cultural and economic spheres continue to strengthen, the Summit seeks to explore the new role that women leaders of "New Asia" can play.

In 2012, the Asia Society and the Lee Kuan Yew School of Public Policy, Singapore plan to launch a research component of the WLNA initiative, which will include a report card on the state of women's leadership in the Asia-Pacific region, along with best practices and country case studies.

Our Research Partner

Headquartered in the Minneapolis metro area, Questar holds a reputation as one of the nation's preeminent research firms **QUESTAR** specializing in employee surveys and organizational research. Established in 1985, we count the country's best-known and largest organizations as clients, across a diverse range of industries. A leader in serving the needs of global organizations by managing the complexities of surveying in differing cultures, languages, and environments, Questar collects data in 74 countries across Europe, Asia, Australia, and North America, in 50 languages, gaining feedback from over 3 million employees worldwide annually. As a product and thought leader, Questar also excels in the development of specialized instruments for accurate and detailed measurement of employee engagement, leadership, and performance improvement.

To have your company participate in the 2012 Asian Pacific Americans Corporate Survey, please contact David Reid at: dreid@AsiaSociety.org

There is no cost to participate.